The Sweater Book

by Hilary Smith Callis

Printed in the United States of America

First Printing, 2015

ISBN 978-1-62767-088-3

Versa Press, Inc
800-447-7829

www.versapress.com

CONTENTS

Introduction

The four sweaters in this book were designed to have interchangeable parts – the neckline shaping, waist shaping, sleeves (or lack thereof), and stitch patterns from each pattern can be applied to any of the other patterns, giving you almost endless garment possibilities. All sweaters are knit from the top down with a construction that makes them easy to adjust for sizing or for other design changes. The patterns can be knit as-is, and modification notes have also been provided throughout each pattern. These let you know the various options for modifications, how to complete them, and take you on an adventure of sweater knitting!

• Converting a closed (pullover) vest or sweater into an open (cardigan) one and vice versa

• Adding sleeves to a vest or omitting sleeves from a sweater

• Changing the length of the sleeves

• Adding a simple cable or lace panel down the back

• Adding a simple cable or lace panel down the front of a pullover or down the front edges of a cardigan

• Changing the type of waist shaping (subtle, emphasized, empire, none)

• Changing the neckline (v-neck, high scoop, deep scoop)

If you would like a sweater different than the specific samples in this book, pick the one closest to what you have in mind, then glance through that pattern to get an idea of how the modifications will work. Begin with the back, cast on, and let the adventure begin!

Hilary

NAPALI CARDIGAN

FINISHED MEASUREMENTS
28.25 (32.5, 36.25, 40.5, 44.25, 48.5, 52.25, 56.5, 60.25, 64.5)" finished bust measurement, buttoned; garment is meant to be worn with 0-2" of negative ease.

YARN
Knit Picks Swish Worsted (100% Superwash Merino Wool; 110 yards/50g):
Indigo Heather 24097, 6 (7, 8, 9, 9, 10, 11, 12, 13, 14) skeins.

NEEDLES
US 7 (4.5mm) 30-60" circular needles (length needed depends on size) and DPNs or two 24" circular needles for two circulars technique, or one 32" or longer circular needle for Magic Loop technique, or size to obtain gauge

NOTIONS
Yarn Needle
4 Stitch Markers
Spare needle, stitch holders, or scrap yarn
10 (10, 11, 11, 11, 11, 11, 11, 12, 12) buttons, 5/8" diameter
Needle and coordinating thread

GAUGE
18 sts and 25 rows = 4" in St st, blocked.
16 sts and 25 rows = 4" in Cellular Stitch lace pattern, blocked.

Napali Cardigan

Notes:

This cardigan features a high scoop neck, subtle waist shaping, long set-in sleeves, and a simple lace pattern adorning the fronts.

The cardigan is worked from the top down, beginning with the back. The fronts are picked up from the CO edge of the back at the shoulders and are knit separately until they are joined to the back at the underarms. After joining, the body is worked in one piece. The sleeves are picked up from the armholes; after the sleeve caps are shaped with short rows, the sleeves are knit in the round down to the sleeve cuffs. The collar edging and button bands are added once the cardigan is complete.

If you are between sizes or wish to modify the bust size for any other reason, you may either add or subtract sts from the CO underarms or the CO sts at the front of the scoop neck, or you may knit the back from one size and the front from another size to customize the fit.

Cellular Stitch (worked flat over a multiple of 3 sts):
Row 1 (RS): K2, *k2tog, yo, k1; rep from * to last st, k1.
Rows 2 and 4 (WS): P to end.
Row 3: K2, *yo, k1, k2tog; rep from * to last st, k1.
To work Cellular Stitch in the round, work Rnds 2 and 4 as: K across.
Rep Rows/Rnds 1-4 for pattern.

Make 1 Left (M1L)
Pick up the bar between st just worked and next st and place on needle as a regular stitch. Knit through the back loop.

Make 1 Right (M1R)
Pick up the bar between st just worked and next st and place on needle backwards (incorrect stitch mount). Knit through the front loop.

Make 1 Purl - Left (M1P-L)
Pick up the bar between st just worked and next st and place on needle backwards (incorrect stitch mount). Purl through the front loop.

Make 1 Purl - Right (M1P-R)
Pick up the bar between st just worked and next st and place on needle as a regular stitch. Purl through the back loop.

Backward Loop Cast On
With needle in your right hand, create a loop by passing the working yarn around your left thumb from back to front. Slip the needle tip under the loop around your thumb. Pull your thumb out of the loop and tug on the working yarn to tighten up the stitch. (For a video demonstration, see http://www.knitpicks.com/tutorials/Loop_Cast_On__D4.html).

Wrap and Turn Short Rows (w&t): Work until the stitch to be wrapped. If knitting: bring yarn to the back of the work, slip next st as if to purl, return the yarn to the front; turn work and slip wrapped st onto right hand needle. Continue across row. If purling: bring yarn to the front of the work, slip next st as if to purl, return the yarn to the back; turn work and slip wrapped st

onto right hand needle. Continue across row.
Picking up wraps: Work to the wrapped st. If knitting, insert the right hand needle under the wrap(s), then through the wrapped st K-wise. Knit the wrap(s) together with the wrapped st. If purling, slip the wrapped st P-wise onto the right hand needle, and use the left hand needle to lift the wrap(s) and place them on the right hand needle. Slip wrap(s) and unworked st back to left hand needle; purl all together through the back loop.

DIRECTIONS

Modification Note: The Back for all four patterns is the same. To modify the neckline, complete the Back, then proceed to the first front in the pattern with the shaping you would like; the Shasta Vest for a v-neck, the Moab Vest for a deep scoop, or the Yuri Pullover for a high scoop worked in the round.

Back

Modification Note: To add a lace panel down the back, CO 2 fewer sts than listed below, mark the center 21 sts, then work Cellular Stitch over those 21 sts until the hem ribbing begins at the bottom of the sweater. To add a cable down the back, CO 2 additional sts, mark the center 12 sts, then work the Shadow Cable from the Yuri Pullover pattern over those 12 sts until the hem ribbing begins.

With longer circular needle, CO 54 (59, 64, 67, 68, 69, 70, 73, 74, 75) sts.
Work in St st for 39 (35, 35, 33, 29, 25, 25, 25, 21, 19) row(s), or until piece measures 6.25 (5.5, 5.5, 5.25, 4.75, 4, 4, 4, 3.25, 3)", beg and ending with a WS row.

Next Row, Armhole Inc Row (RS): K1, M1R, k to last st, M1L, k1. 2 sts inc'd.
Working in St st, rep Armhole Inc Row every 4th row 0 (2, 3, 2, 2, 2, 2, 2, 1, 1) time(s), then every other row 2 (2, 2, 5, 8, 10, 12, 12, 17, 21) times.

Last Armhole Inc Row (WS): P1, M1P-R, p to last st, M1P-L, p1. 2 sts inc'd. 62 (71, 78, 85, 92, 97, 102, 105, 114, 123) sts.

Break yarn and place Back sts on spare needle, st holder, or scrap yarn.

Modification Note: If you would like to knit a pullover version of this sweater, proceed to the Left Front in the Yuri Pullover pattern, then follow the instructions in that pattern until you have joined the fronts to the back. Come back to this pattern for the Body after the joining row.

Right Front

With RS of Back facing, starting at the top right edge, and using longer circular needle, pick up 6 (8, 10, 11, 11, 11, 12, 12, 13, 13) sts from the CO edge.

Work in St st for 1 (3, 3, 3, 3, 3, 3, 3, 3) row(s), beg and ending with a WS row.

Note: Please read the rest of this section in its entirety before proceeding and refer to the instructions broken down by size below to determine when to start the armhole shaping.
For Sizes 60.25" and 64.5", the armhole and high scoop neck are shaped at the same time.

Sizes 28.25 (32.5, 36.25, 40.5, 44.25, 48.5, 52.25, 56.5, -, -)":
After High Scoop Neck Shaping is complete, work 21 (15, 15, 11, 7, 1, 1, 1, -, -) row(s) in pat as set for Lace Panel below, then proceed to Armhole Shaping.

Sizes 60.25" and 64.5":
Begin Armhole Shaping on the same row as the - (-, -, -, -, -, -, -, 10th, 9th) High Scoop increase.

High Scoop Neck Shaping
Next Row, High Scoop Inc Row (RS): K to last st, M1L, k1. 1 st inc'd. Working in St st (and incorporating armhole shaping if applicable when the time comes), rep High Scoop Inc Row every 4th row 0 (0, 0, 0, 0, 1, 1, 0, 0, 0) more time(s), then every other row 7 (7, 7, 8, 8, 7, 7, 9, 9, 9) times.

Last High Scoop Inc Row (WS): P1, M1P-R, p to end. 1 st inc'd.

Modification Note: For plain fronts without lace, CO 1 additional st on the next row. To add a cable to the front edge instead of lace, CO 3 additional sts on the next row, mark the last 12 sts of the row, and work the Shadow Cable from the Yuri Pullover pattern over those sts until the hem ribbing begins.

Next Row (RS): K to end (incorporating armhole shaping if necessary), then CO 9 (10, 10, 10, 10, 11, 10, 11, 10, 11) sts using the Backward Loop Method. Total sts (including armhole shaping, if applicable): 24 (27, 29, 31, 31, 33, 33, 35, 36, 38).

Set Up Lace Panel:
Next Row (WS): P12, pm, p to end.
Next Row (RS), begin lace: K to marker (incorporating armhole shaping if necessary), sm, work Cellular Stitch to end, beg with Row 1.

Cont working Cellular Stitch over the last 12 sts of the Right Front for the rest of the cardigan body until the hem ribbing begins.

Armhole Shaping
Armhole Inc Row (RS): K1, M1R, work in pat as set to end (incorporating high scoop shaping if applicable). 1 st inc'd. Working in pat and incorporating high scoop shaping as necessary, rep Armhole Inc Row every 4th row 0 (2, 3, 2, 2, 2, 2, 2, 1, 1) more time(s), then every other row 2 (2, 2, 5, 8, 10, 12, 12, 17, 21) times.

Last Armhole Inc Row (WS): Work in pat to last st, M1P-L, p1. 1 st inc'd. 28 (33, 36, 40, 43, 46, 48, 50, 54, 59) sts.

Break yarn and place Right Front sts on spare needle, st holder, or scrap yarn.

Left Front
With RS of Back facing, count to the 6 (8, 10, 11, 11, 11, 12, 12, 13, 13)th st from the top left edge. Starting here, with longer circular needle, pick up 6 (8, 10, 11, 11, 11, 12, 12, 13, 13) sts from the CO edge.

Work in St st for 1 (3, 3, 3, 3, 3, 3, 3, 3, 3) rows, beg and ending with a WS row.

Note: Please read the rest of this section in its entirety before proceeding and refer to the instructions broken down by size below to determine when to start the armhole shaping.

For Sizes 60.25" and 64.5", the armhole and high scoop neck are shaped at the same time.

Sizes 28.25 (32.5, 36.25, 40.5, 44.25, 48.5, 52.25, 56.5, -, -)":
After High Scoop Neck Shaping is complete, work 22 (16, 16, 12, 8, 2, 2, 2, -, -), rows in pat as set for Lace Panel below, then proceed to Armhole Shaping.

Sizes 60.25" and 64.5"
Begin Armhole Shaping on the same row as the - (-, -, -, -, -, -, -, 10th, 9th) High Scoop increase.

High Scoop Neck Shaping:
Next Row, High Scoop Inc Row (RS): K1, M1R, k to end. 1 st inc'd. Working in St st (and incorporating armhole shaping if applicable when the time comes), rep High Scoop Inc Row every 4th row 0 (0, 0, 0, 0, 1, 1, 0, 0, 0) more time(s), then every other row 7 (7, 7, 8, 8, 7, 7, 9, 9, 9) times.

Modification Note: For plain fronts without lace, CO 1 additional st on the next row on the next row. To add a cable to the front edge instead of lace, CO 3 additional sts on the next row, mark the first 12 sts of the next RS row, and work the Shadow Cable from the Yuri Pullover pattern over those sts until the hem ribbing begins.

Last High Scoop Inc Row (WS): P to last st, M1P-L, p1, then CO 9 (10, 10, 10, 10, 11, 10, 11, 10, 11) sts using the Backward Loop method. 24 (27, 29, 31, 31, 33, 33, 35, 36, 37) sts (including armhole shaping, if applicable).

Next Row (RS): K to end (incorporating armhole shaping if necessary).

Set Up Lace Panel:
Next Row (WS): P to last 12 sts, pm, p12.
Next Row (RS), begin lace: Work in Cellular Stitch to marker, beg with Row 1, sm, then k to end (incorporating armhole shaping if necessary).

Cont working Cellular Stitch over the first 12 sts of the Left Front for the rest of the cardigan body until the hem ribbing begins.

Armhole Shaping
Armhole Inc Row (RS): Work in pat as set to to last st (incorporating high scoop shaping if necessary), M1L, k1. 1 st inc'd. Working in pat and incorporating High Scoop Inc Rows as necessary, rep Armhole Inc Row every 4th row 0 (2, 3, 2, 2, 2, 2, 2, 1, 1) more time(s), then every other row 2 (2, 2, 5, 8, 10, 12, 12, 17, 21) times.

Last Armhole Inc Row (WS): P1, M1P-R, work in pat to end. 1 st inc'd. 28 (33, 36, 40, 43, 46, 48, 50, 54, 59) sts.

Leave sts on your needle and do not break yarn.

Body
Join Fronts and Back (RS): Work in pat to end of Left Front, CO 1 (1, 2, 3, 4, 6, 8, 11, 11, 11) st(s) using Backward Loop Method, pm, CO 1 (1, 2, 3, 4, 6, 8, 11, 11, 11) more st(s), place sts of Back onto left hand needle, k to end of Back, CO 1 (1, 2, 3, 4, 6, 8, 11, 11, 11) st(s) using Backward Loop Method, pm, CO 1 (1, 2, 3, 4, 6, 8, 11, 11, 11) more st(s), place sts of Right Front onto left hand needle, and work in pat to end of Right Front. 122 (141, 158, 177, 194, 213, 230, 249, 266, 285) sts.

Modification Note: To alter the waist shaping, see the Body instructions in the Moab Vest pattern (for no waist shaping), the Shasta Vest pattern (for a slightly more emphasized waist), or the Yuri Pullover pattern (for an empire waist). If working in the round, replace the Waist Dec Rows below with the Waist Dec Rnd from the Shasta Vest or Yuri Pullover patterns.

Work in pat as set, with the first and last 12 sts in Cellular Stitch and the rest in St st, until Body measures 3.5 (3.5, 3.5, 3.5, 3.5, 3.5, 3.75, 3.75, 3.75, 3.75)" from underarm, ending with a WS row.

Next Row, Waist Dec Row (RS): Work in pat to 2 sts before second marker, k2tog, sm, k1, ssk, knit to 2 sts before next marker, k2tog, sm, k1, ssk, then work in pat to end. 4 sts dec'd.

Working in pat, rep Waist Dec Row again when Body measures 7 (7, 7.25, 7.25, 7.25, 7.25, 7.5, 7.5, 7.5, 7.5)" from underarm. 114 (133, 150, 169, 186, 205, 222, 241, 258, 277) sts.

Work in pat for 5 rows.

Next Row, Hip Inc Row (RS): Work in pat to marker, M1L, sm, k1, M1R, knit to next marker, M1L, sm, k1, M1R, work in pat to end. 4 sts inc'd.

Work in pat for 2.5", ending with a WS row, then rep Hip Inc Row. 122 (141, 158, 177, 194, 213, 230, 249, 266, 285) sts.

Work in pat until Body measures 13 (13, 13.25, 13.25, 13.25, 13.25, 13.5, 13.5, 13.5, 13.5)", or 1 (1, 1, 1, 1.25, 1.25, 1.25, 1.25, 1.5, 1.5)" less than desired length from underarm, ending with a WS row. On last row, inc 0 (2, 0, 2, 0, 2, 0, 2, 0, 2) st(s) anywhere in the row with M1L-P to make the st count compatible with the hem ribbing. 122 (143, 158, 179, 194, 215, 230, 251, 266, 287) sts.

Hem Ribbing (RS): *K2, p1; rep from * to last 2 sts, k2.
Work in ribbing pat as set in last row until ribbing measures 1 (1, 1, 1, 1.25, 1.25, 1.25, 1.25, 1.5, 1.5)", ending with a WS row.

BO all sts knitwise.

Sleeves (make 2)

Modification Note: For plain 3/4 length sleeves, follow the instructions below up to the first Sleeve Dec Rnd, then follow the Sleeve instructions in the Yuri Pullover pattern beg with the first Sleeve Dec Rnd and omitting the very last Sleeve Dec Rnd. For cabled sleeves, see the Sleeve instructions in the Yuri Pullover pattern. To leave off the sleeves, see Armhole Edging in the Simple or Moab Vest patterns.

Starting in the very center of the underarm and using needles preferred for working a small circumference in the round, PU 1 (1, 2, 3, 4, 6, 8, 11, 11, 11) st(s) from CO underarm sts, 22 (24, 26, 28, 29, 31, 31, 30, 32, 35) sts up the armhole to where the Front meets the Back at the shoulder, pm, PU 22 (24, 26, 28, 29, 31, 31, 30, 32, 35) sts down the armhole to the underarm, then PU 1 (1, 2, 3, 4, 6, 8, 11, 11, 11) more st(s) from the CO underarm sts. 46 (50, 56, 62, 66, 74, 78, 82, 86, 92) sts. Pm to mark beg of rnd, then join to work in the rnd.

You will now shape the sleeve cap with short rows.

Row 1 (RS): K to 1st marker, sm, k6 (7, 8, 8, 9, 9, 9, 9, 10, 11), w&t.

Row 2 (WS): P to 1st marker, sm, p6 (7, 8, 8, 9, 9, 9, 9, 10, 11), w&t.
Row 3: K to wrapped st, slipping marker as you come to it, k wrap together with st, w&t.
Row 4: P to wrapped st, slipping marker as you come to it, p wrap together with st, w&t.

Rep Rows 3 and 4 until 0 (0, 2, 4, 6, 10, 14, 20, 20, 20) underarm sts remain between last two wrapped sts.

Next Row (RS): K to end of rnd, removing 1st marker and knitting wrap together with st near the end of the rnd when you come to it.

Next Rnd: K to end, knitting last wrap together with st near the beg of the rnd as you come to it.

Work in St st until sleeve measures 2" from underarm at beg of rnd marker.

Next Rnd, Sleeve Dec Rnd: K1, ssk, k to 2 sts from end, k2tog. 2 sts dec'd.

Working in St st, rep Sleeve Dec Rnd every 12 (10, 7, 8, 7, 5, 6, 5, 6, 5)th rnd 4 (3, 12, 3, 3, 18, 5, 14, 3, 9) times, then every 11 (9, -, 7, 6, -, 5, 4, 5, 4)th rnd 3 (6, -, 9, 11, -, 12, 5, 15, 12) times. 30 (30, 30, 36, 36, 36, 42, 42, 48, 48) sts.

Work in St st until sleeve measures 15.5 (16, 16, 16.5, 16.5, 17, 17, 17, 17.5, 17.5)" from underarm.

Cuff Ribbing: *K2, p1; rep from * to end.
Work in ribbing pat as set in last rnd until ribbing measures 1".

BO all sts knitwise.

Scoop Neck Edging

Modification Note: To add a turtleneck or large collar, see Turtleneck instructions in the Yuri Pullover pattern.

Beg at the top of the right front edge with RS facing and using longer circular needle, PU 1 st for each st CO and roughly 3 sts for every 4 rows all the way around the neck opening. The exact number of sts is not important, but it should be a multiple of 3 plus 2.

Next Row (WS): *P2, k1; rep from * to last 2 sts, p2.
Work in ribbing pat as set in last row for 2 more rows.

BO all sts knitwise.

Left Button Band

Beg at the top of the left front opening with RS facing and using longer circular needle, PU 89 (89, 95, 95, 95, 95, 98, 98, 104, 104) sts down the cardigan opening. This will be roughly 3 sts picked up for every 4 rows. (Note: If you have adjusted the length of the cardigan, you may have a different number of sts. Make sure it is a multiple of 3 sts plus 2.)

Next Row (WS): *P2, k1; rep from * to last 2 sts, p2.

Work in ribbing pat as set in last row for 2 more rows.

BO all sts knitwise.

Right Button Band

Modification Note: If you have done a Deep Scoop Neck or have shortened (or lengthened) the distance between the scoop neck and the hem at all, the number of sts picked up will be different than below, and the number of buttons used and the spacing of the buttonholes will need to be altered. In this case, decide how many buttons you would like to use, then evenly space the same number of buttonholes within the Right Button Band.

Beg at the bottom of the right front opening with RS facing and using longer circular needle, PU 89 (89, 95, 95, 95, 95, 98, 98, 104, 104) sts up the cardigan opening. This will be roughly 3 sts picked up for every 4 rows. (Note: If you have adjusted the length of the cardigan, pick up the same number of sts that you picked up for the Left Button Band.)

Next Row (WS): *P1, p2tog, yo, [p2, k1] 2 times; rep from * to 17 (17, 14, 14, 14, 14, 17, 17, 14, 14) sts from end, p1, p2tog, yo, [p2, k1] 3 (3, 2, 2, 2, 2, 3, 3, 2, 2) times, p1, p2tog, yo, p2.

Next Row (RS): *K2, p1; rep from * to last 2 sts, k2.

Work in ribbing pat as set in last row for 1 more row.

BO all sts knitwise.

Finishing

Weave in ends, wash and block to measurements in schematic. Sew buttons to Left Button Band at same intervals as buttonholes.

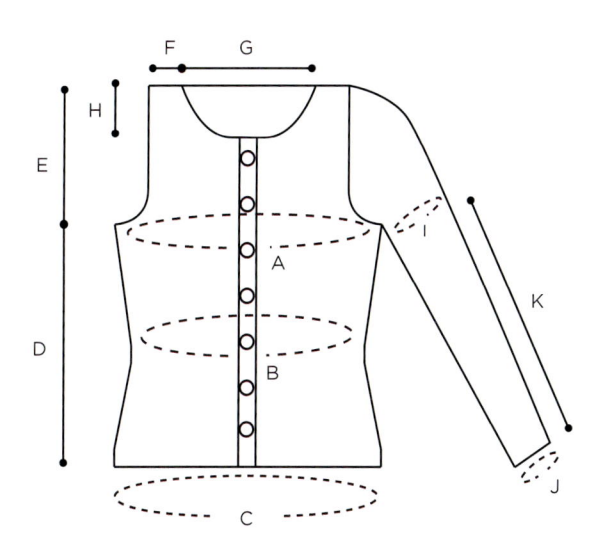

A 28.25 (32.5, 36.25, 40.5, 44.25, 48.5, 52.25, 56.5, 60.25, 64.5)"
B 26.5 (30.75, 34.5, 38.75, 42.5, 46.75, 50.5, 54.75, 58.5, 62.75)"
C 28.25 (32.5, 36.25, 40.5, 44.25, 48.5, 52.25, 56.5, 60.25, 64.5)"
D 14 (14, 14.25, 14.25, 14.5, 14.5, 14.75, 14.75, 15, 15)"
E 7.25 (8, 8.75, 8.75, 9, 9, 9.5, 9.5, 10, 11)"
F 1.25 (1.75, 2.25, 2.5, 2.5, 2.5, 2.75, 2.75, 3, 3)"
G 9.25 (9.5, 9.75, 10, 10.25, 10.5, 10.25, 11, 10.75, 11)"
H 3 (3.25, 3.25, 3.5, 3.5, 3.75, 3.75, 3.75, 3.75, 3.75)"
I 10.25 (11.25, 12.5, 13.75, 14.75, 16.5, 17.25, 18.25, 19.25, 20.5)"
J 6.75 (6.75, 6.75, 8, 8, 8, 9.25, 9.25, 10.75, 10.75)"
K 16.5 (17, 17, 17.5, 17.5, 18, 18, 18, 18.5, 18.5)"

YURI PULLOVER

FINISHED MEASUREMENTS

28.5 (32.5, 36.5, 40.5, 44.5, 48.5, 52.5, 56.5, 60.5, 64.5)" finished bust measurement; garment is meant to be worn with 0-2" of negative ease.

YARN

Knit Picks Swish Worsted (100% Superwash Merino Wool; 110 yards/50g):
Delft Heather 24095, 8 (9, 10, 11, 12, 13, 14, 15, 17, 18) skeins.

NEEDLES

US 7 (4.5mm) 24-60" circular needles (length needed depends on size), 24" circular needles (for collar), and DPNs or two 24" circular needles for two circulars technique, or one 32" or longer circular needle for Magic Loop technique, or size to obtain gauge

NOTIONS

Cable Needle
Yarn Needle
2 Stitch Markers
Spare needle, stitch holders, or scrap yarn

GAUGE

18 sts and 25 rows = 4" in St st worked in the round, blocked.
22 sts and 26 rows = 4" in Shadow Cable pattern, blocked.

Yuri Pullover

Notes:

This pullover features a high scoop neck with an added turtleneck, empire waist shaping, and three-quarters length sleeves with a simple cable pattern adorning them.

The sweater is worked from the top down, beginning with the back. The fronts are picked up from the CO edge of the back at the shoulders and are knit separately until they are joined at the bottom of the high scoop neck. The front and back are joined at the underarms, after which the body is worked in the round in one piece. The sleeves are picked up from the armholes; after the sleeve caps are shaped with short rows, the sleeves are knit in the round down to the sleeve cuffs. The turtleneck is added once the body of the sweater is complete.

If you are between sizes or wish to modify the bust size for any other reason, you may either add or subtract sts from the CO underarms or the CO sts at the front of the scoop neck, or you may knit the back from one size and the front from another size to customize the fit.

Shadow Cable (worked over 12 sts):
Row 1 (RS): K4, c2 over 2 right, k4.
Row 2 and all even rows (WS): P.
Row 3: K3, c2 over 1 right, c2 over 1 left, k3.
Row 5: K2, c2 over 1 right, k2, c2 over 1 left, k2.
Row 7: K1, c2 over 1 right, k4, c2 over 1 left, k1.
To work the Shadow Cable Pattern in the round, work even rounds as: K across.
Rep Rows/Rnds 1-8 for pattern.

C2 over 2 Right: Sl 2 to CN, hold in back. K2, k2 from CN.

C2 over 1 Right: Sl 1 to CN, hold in back. K2, k1 from CN.

C2 over 1 Left: Sl 2 to CN, hold in front. K1, k2 from CN.

Make 1 Left (M1L)
Pick up the bar between st just worked and next st and place on needle as a regular stitch. Knit through the back loop.

Make 1 Right (M1R)
Pick up the bar between st just worked and next st and place on needle backwards (incorrect stitch mount). Knit through the front loop.

Make 1 Purl - Left (M1P-L)
Pick up the bar between st just worked and next st and place on needle backwards (incorrect stitch mount). Purl through the front loop.

Make 1 Purl - Right (M1P-R)
Pick up the bar between st just worked and next st and place on needle as a regular stitch. Purl through the back loop.

Backward Loop Cast On
With needle in your right hand, create a loop by passing the working yarn around your left thumb from back to front. Slip the needle tip under the loop around your thumb. Pull your thumb out of the loop and tug on the working yarn to tighten up the stitch. (For a video demonstration, see http://www.knitpicks.com/tutorials/Loop_Cast_On__D4.html).

Wrap and Turn Short Rows (w&t): Work until the stitch to be wrapped. If knitting: bring yarn to the back of the work, slip next st as if to purl, return the yarn to the front; turn work and slip wrapped st onto right hand needle. Continue across row. If purling: bring yarn to the front of the work, slip next st as if to purl, return the yarn to the back; turn work and slip wrapped st onto right hand needle. Continue across row.
Picking up wraps: Work to the wrapped st. If knitting, insert the right hand needle under the wrap(s), then through the wrapped st K-wise. Knit the wrap(s) together with the wrapped st. If purling, slip the wrapped st P-wise onto the right hand needle, and use the left hand needle to lift the wrap(s) and place them on the right hand needle. Slip wrap(s) and unworked st back to left hand needle; purl all together through the back loop.

DIRECTIONS

Modification Note: The Back for all four patterns is the same. To modify the neckline, complete the Back, then proceed to the first front in the pattern with the shaping you would like: the Shasta Vest for a V-neck, the Moab Vest for a deep scoop, or the Napali Cardigan for a high scoop worked flat.

Back

Modification Note: To add a lace panel down the back, CO 2 fewer sts than listed below, mark the center 21 sts, then work Cellular Stitch from the Napali Cardigan pattern over those 21 sts until the hem ribbing begins at the bottom of the sweater. To add a cable down the back, CO 2 additional sts, mark the center 12 sts, then work the Shadow Cable over those 12 sts until the hem ribbing begins.

With longer circular needle, CO 54 (59, 64, 67, 68, 69, 70, 73, 74, 75) sts.
Work in St st (K on RS, P on WS) for 39 (35, 35, 33, 29, 25, 25, 25, 21, 19) rows, or until piece measures 6.25 (5.5, 5.5, 5.25, 4.75, 4, 4, 4, 3.25, 3)" beg and ending with a WS row.

Next Row, Armhole Inc Row (RS): K1, M1R, k to last st, M1L, k1. 2 sts inc'd.
Working in St st, rep Armhole Inc Row every 4th row 0 (2, 3, 2, 2, 2, 2, 2, 1, 1) more time(s), then every other row 2 (2, 2, 5, 8, 10, 12, 12, 17, 21) times. 60 (69, 76, 83, 90, 95, 100, 103, 112, 121) sts.

Last Armhole Inc Row (WS): P1, M1P-R, p to last st, M1P-L, p1. 2 sts inc'd. 62 (71, 78, 85, 92, 97, 102, 105, 114, 123) sts.

Break yarn and place Back sts on spare needle, st holder, or scrap yarn.

Modification Note: If you would like to knit a cardigan version of this sweater, proceed to the Right Front in the Napali Cardigan pattern, then follow the instructions in that pattern until you have joined the fronts to the back. Come back to this pattern for the Body after the joining row.

Left Front

With RS of Back facing, count to the 6 (8, 10, 11, 11, 11, 12, 12, 13, 13)th st from the top left edge. Starting here, with longer circular needle, pick up 6 (8, 10, 11, 11, 11, 12, 12, 13, 13) sts from the CO edge.

Work in St st for 1 (3, 3, 3, 3, 3, 3, 3, 3) row(s), beg and ending with a WS row.

Note: For Sizes 60.5" and 64.5", the armhole shaping begins a few rows before High Scoop Neck shaping ends. Please read the rest of this section in its entirety before proceeding.

High Scoop Neck Shaping

Next Row, High Scoop Inc Row (RS): K1, M1R, k to end. 1 st inc'd. Working in St st (and incorporating armhole shaping if applicable when the time comes), rep High Scoop Inc Row every 4th row 0 (0, 0, 0, 0, 1, 1, 0, 0) more time(s), then every other row 7 (7, 7, 8, 8, 7, 7, 9, 9, 9) times.

Last High Scoop Inc Row (WS): P to last st, M1P-L, p1. 15 (17, 19, 21, 21, 21, 22, 23, 25, 25) including armhole shaping, if applicable.

Sizes 60.5" and 64.5" ONLY:
Armhole Shaping

AT THE SAME TIME, beg armhole shaping on the same row as the - (-, -, -, -, -, -, -, 10th, 9th) High Scoop Inc Row.

Armhole Inc Row (RS): Work in pat as set to to last st (incorporating high scoop shaping if necessary), M1L, k1. 1 st inc'd. Work - (-, -, -, -, -, -, -, 1, 3) row(s) in St st, incorporating high scoop shaping where necessary.

All Sizes

Break yarn and place Left Front sts on spare needle, st holder, or scrap yarn.

Right Front

With RS of Back facing, starting at the top right edge, and using longer circular needle, pick up 6 (8, 10, 11, 11, 11, 12, 12, 13, 13) sts from the CO edge.

Work in St st for 1 (3, 3, 3, 3, 3, 3, 3, 3) row(s), beg and ending with a WS row.

Note: For Sizes 60.5" and 64.5", the armhole shaping begins a few rows before High Scoop Neck shaping ends. Please read the rest of this section in its entirety before proceeding.

High Scoop Neck Shaping

Next Row, High Scoop Inc Row (RS): K to last st, M1L, k1. 1 st inc'd. Working in St st (and incorporating armhole shaping if applicable when the time comes), rep High Scoop Inc Row every 4th row 0 (0, 0, 0, 0, 1, 1, 0, 0) more time(s), then every other row 7 (7, 7, 8, 8, 7, 7, 9, 9, 9) times.

Last High Scoop Inc Row (WS): P1, M1P-R, p to end. 15 (17, 19, 21, 21, 21, 22, 23, 25, 25) sts including armhole shaping, if applicable.

Sizes 60.5" and 64.5" ONLY:
Armhole Shaping

AT THE SAME TIME, beg armhole shaping on the same row as the - (-, -, -, -, -, -, -, 10th, 9th) High Scoop Inc Row.

Armhole Inc Row (RS): K1, M1R, work in pat as set to end (incorporating high scoop shaping if applicable). 1 st inc'd. Work - (-, -, -, -, -, -, -, 1, 3) row(s) in St st, incorporating high scoop shaping where necessary.

All Sizes

Leave sts on your needle and do not break yarn.

Front

Modification Note: To add a lace panel down the front of this pullover, CO 2 fewer sts on the next row. Place markers on either side of the center 21 sts, then work Cellular Stitch from the Napali Cardigan pattern over those marked 21 sts until the hem ribbing begins. To add a cable down the front of the pullover, CO 2 additional sts in the next row, then mark the center 12 sts and work the Shadow Cable over those sts until the hem ribbing begins.

Note: For size 64.5" ONLY, the next row is also an Armhole Inc row. For that size, add a M1R after the first st of the Right Front and a M1L before the last st of the left front.

Next Row (RS): Join Right and Left Front: K to end of Right Front, CO 24 (25, 26, 25, 26, 27, 26, 27, 26, 27) sts using Backward Loop method, place sts of Left Front onto left hand needle, k to end. 54 (59, 64, 67, 68, 69, 70, 73, 76, 79) sts.

Work 21 (15, 15, 11, 7, 1, 1, 1, 1, 1) row(s) in St st, beg and ending with a WS row.

Next Row, Armhole Inc Row (RS): K1, M1R, k to last st, M1L, k1. 2 sts inc'd. Working in St st, rep Armhole Inc Row every 4th row 0 (2, 3, 2, 2, 2, 2, 2, 0, 0) more times, then every other row 2 (2, 2, 5, 8, 10, 12, 12, 17, 20) times. 62 (71, 78, 85, 92, 97, 102, 105, 114, 123) sts.

Last Armhole Inc Row (WS): P1, M1P-R, p to last st, M1P-L, p1. 2 sts inc'd. 62 (71, 78, 85, 92, 97, 102, 105, 114, 123) sts.

Body

Join Front and Back (RS): K to end of Front, CO 1 (1, 2, 3, 4, 6, 8, 11, 11, 11) st(s) using Backward Loop Method, pm, CO 1 (1, 2, 3, 4, 6, 8, 11, 11, 11) more st(s), place sts of Back onto left hand needle, k to end of Back, CO 1 (1, 2, 3, 4, 6, 8, 11, 11, 11) st(s) using Backward Loop Method, pm to mark beg of rnd, CO 1 (1, 2, 3, 4, 6, 8, 11, 11, 11) more st(s), and join to work in the rnd. 128 (146, 164, 182, 200, 218, 236, 254, 272, 290) sts.

Modification Note: To alter the waist shaping, see the Body instructions in the Moab Vest pattern (for no waist shaping), the Napali Cardigan pattern (for a subtle standard waist) or the Shasta Vest pattern (for a slightly more emphasized waist). If working flat, replace the Waist Dec Rnds below with the Waist Dec Row from the Napali Cardigan pattern.

Work in St st for 10 rnds, or until piece measures 1.75 (1.75, 1.75, 1.75, 1.75, 1.75, 1.75, 1.5, 1.5, 1.5)" from underarm.

Next Rnd, Waist Dec Rnd: *K1, ssk, k to 2 sts before marker, k2tog, sm; rep from * once more. 4 sts dec'd.

Working in St st, rep Waist Dec Rnd again when Body measures 3.75 (3.75, 3.75, 3.5, 3.5, 3.5, 3.5, 3.25, 3.25, 3.25)" from underarm. 120 (138, 156, 174, 192, 210, 228, 246, 264, 282) sts.

Work in St st for 5 rnds.

Next Rnd, Hip Inc Rnd: *K1, M1R, k to marker, M1L, sm; rep from * once more. 4 sts inc'd.

Working in St st, rep Hip Inc Rnd every 14th rnd 4 (4, 3, 3, 3, 2,

1, 1, 1) time(s), then every 16th rnd 0 (0, 1, 1, 1, 1, 2, 3, 3, 3) time(s). 140 (158, 176, 194, 212, 230, 248, 266, 284, 302) sts.

Work in St st until Body measures 14.5 (14.5, 14.75, 14.75, 14.75, 14.75, 15, 15, 15, 15)", or 1.5 (1.5, 1.5, 1.5, 1.75, 1.75, 1.75, 1.75, 2, 2)" less than desired length from underarm. On last rnd, inc 1 st anywhere in the rnd with M1L to make the st count compatible with the hem ribbing. 141 (159, 177, 195, 213, 231, 249, 267, 285, 303) sts.

Hem Ribbing: *K2, p1; rep from * to end.
Work in ribbing pat as set in last rnd until ribbing measures 1.5 (1.5, 1.5, 1.5, 1.75, 1.75, 1.75, 1.75, 2, 2)".

BO all sts knitwise.

Sleeves (make 2)

Modification Note: For long cabled sleeves, follow the instructions below up to the first Sleeve Dec Rnd, then follow the Sleeve instructions in the Napali Cardigan pattern beg with the first Sleeve Dec Rnd and adding 2 sts just before the first rnd of cuff ribbing. For plain sleeves, see the Sleeve instructions in the Napali Cardigan pattern. To leave off the sleeves, see Armhole Edging in the Simple or Moab Vest patterns.

Starting in the very center of the underarm and using needles preferred for working a small circumference in the round, PU 1 (1, 2, 3, 4, 6, 8, 11, 11, 11) st(s) from CO underarm sts, 23 (25, 27, 29, 30, 32, 32, 31, 33, 36) sts up the armhole to where the Front meets the Back at the shoulder, pm, PU 23 (25, 27, 29, 30, 32, 32, 31, 33, 36) sts down the armhole to the underarm, then PU 1 (1, 2, 3, 4, 6, 8, 11, 11, 11) more st(s) from the CO underarm sts. Total sts: 48 (52, 58, 64, 68, 76, 80, 84, 88, 94). Pm to mark beg of rnd, then join to work in the rnd.

You will now shape the sleeve cap with short rows and will begin the cable pat that will run down the length of the sleeve.

Row 1 (RS): K to 6 sts before marker, pm, work Row 1 of Shadow Cable (using written instructions or Chart A) over next 12 sts, removing marker as you come to it, pm, k0 (1, 2, 2, 3, 3, 3, 3, 4, 5), w&t.

Cont working the Shadow Cable pat over the 12 sts between the 2 markers placed in the last row until the cuff ribbing begins.

Row 2 (WS): Work in pat to 2nd marker, sm, p0 (1, 2, 2, 3, 3, 3, 3, 4, 5), w&t.
Row 3: Work in pat to wrapped st, slipping markers as you come to them, k wrap together with st, w&t.
Row 4: Work in pat to wrapped st, slipping markers as you come to them, p wrap together with st, w&t.

Rep Rows 3 and 4 until 0 (0, 2, 4, 6, 10, 14, 20, 20, 20) underarm sts remain between last two wrapped sts.

Next Row (RS): Work to end of rnd, knitting wrap together with st near the end of the rnd when you come to it.

Next Rnd: Work to end, knitting last wrap together with st near the beg of the rnd as you come to it.

Work in pat until sleeve measures 2" from underarm at beg of rnd marker.

Next Rnd, Sleeve Dec Rnd: K1, ssk, work to 2 sts from end, k2tog. 2 sts dec'd.

Working in pat, rep Sleeve Dec Rnd every 12 (9, 9, 6, 7, 5, 6, 5, 5, 5)th rnd 1 (1, 1, 10, 6, 10, 2, 6, 13, 1) more time(s), then every 11 (8, 8, 5, 6, 4, 5, 4, 0, 4)th rnd 4 (6, 6, 0, 3, 3, 10, 8, 0, 15) times. 36 (36, 42, 42, 48, 48, 54, 54, 60, 60) sts.

Work in pat until sleeve measures 11.5 (11.75, 11.75, 12.25, 12.25, 12.5, 12.5, 12.5, 13, 13)" from underarm.

Cuff Ribbing: *K2, p1; rep from * to end.
Work in ribbing pat as set in last rnd until ribbing measures 1".

BO all sts knitwise.

Turtleneck

Modification Note: To add a large collar to a cardigan or open-fronted vest, pick up a multiple of 3 sts plus 2 around the neck opening, then work the ribbing pattern flat (as for the High Scoop Neck Edging in the Napali Cardigan pattern) for 9", or to desired length.

Beg at the top of the right front edge with RS facing and using 24" circular needles, PU 1 st for each st CO and roughly 3 sts for every 4 rows all the way around the neck opening. The exact number of sts is not important, but it should be a multiple of 3. Pm to mark beg of rnd, then join to work in the rnd.

Rib Rnd: *K2, p1; rep from * to end.
Work in ribbing pat as set in last rnd until Turtleneck measures 9" when slightly stretched to simulate blocking (or desired length).

BO all sts knitwise.

Finishing
Weave in ends, wash and block to measurements in schematic.

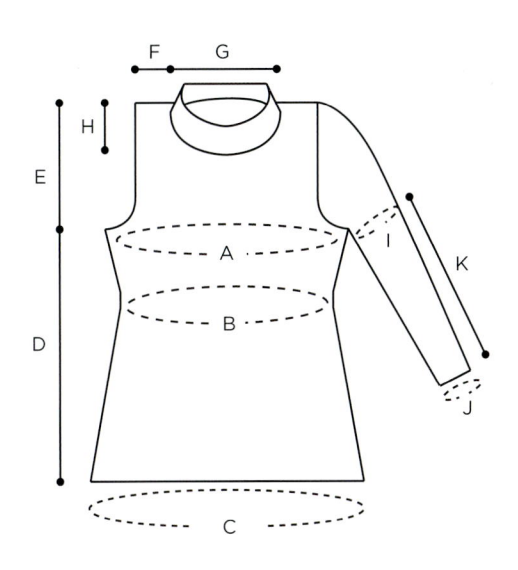

A 28.5 (32.5, 36.5, 40.5, 44.5, 48.5, 52.5, 56.5, 60.5, 64.5)"
B 26.75 (30.75, 34.75, 38.75, 42.75, 46.75, 50.75, 54.75, 58.75, 62.75)"
C 31.25 (35.25, 39.25, 43.25, 47.25, 51.25, 55.25, 59.25, 63.25, 67.25)"
D 16 (16, 16.25, 16.25, 16.5, 16.5, 16.75, 16.75, 17, 17)"
E 7.25 (8, 8.75, 8.75, 9, 9, 9.5, 9.5, 10, 11)"
F 1.25 (1.75, 2.25, 2.5, 2.5, 2.5, 2.75, 2.75, 3, 3)"
G 9.25 (9.5, 9.75, 10, 10.25, 10.5, 10.25, 11, 10.75, 11)"
H 3 (3.25, 3.25, 3.5, 3.5, 3.75, 3.75, 3.75, 3.75, 3.75)"
I 10.25 (11, 12.5, 13.75, 14.75, 16.5, 17.25, 18.25, 19, 20.5)"
J 7.5 (7.5, 9, 9, 10.25, 10.25, 11.5, 11.5, 13, 13)"
K 12.5 (12.75, 12.75, 13.25, 13.25, 13.5, 13.5, 13.5, 14, 14)"

Note: The turtleneck extends 9" up from the collar opening.

Chart A: Shadow Cable, worked in the round or flat

12	11	10	9	8	7	6	5	4	3	2	1	
												8
	⅄		⅄				⅄		⅄			7
												6
		⅄		⅄		⅄		⅄				5
												4
			⅄		⅄⅄		⅄					3
												2
				⅄ ⅄								1

Legend

☐ **knit**
knit on RS or when working in the rnd
purl on WS when working flat

c2 over 2 right
sl2 to CN, hold in back.
k2, k2 from CN

c2 over 1 right
sl1 to CN, hold in back.
k2, k1 from CN

c2 over 1 left
sl2 to CN, hold in front.
k1, k2 from CN

MOAB VEST

FINISHED MEASUREMENTS

28.5 (32.5, 36.5, 40.5, 44.5, 48.5, 52.5, 56.5, 60.5, 64.5)" finished bust measurement with vest closed and overlapped by 4.5"; garment is meant to be worn open with 0-2" of negative ease across the back.

YARN

Knit Picks Swish Worsted (100% Superwash Merino Wool; 110 yards/50g):
Lava Heather 24295, 5 (5, 6, 7, 7, 8, 9, 9, 10, 10) skeins.

NEEDLES

US 7 (4.5mm) 30-60" circular needles (length needed depends on size) and DPNs or two 24" circular needles for two circulars technique, or one 32" or longer circular needle for Magic Loop technique, or size to obtain gauge

NOTIONS

Yarn Needle
Spare needle, stitch holders, or scrap yarn

GAUGE

18 sts and 25 rows = 4" in St st and Textured Stitch Pattern, blocked.

Moab Vest

Notes:

This vest features a simple textured stitch pattern throughout, deep scoop neck shaping, and a straight body with no waist shaping.

The vest is worked from the top down, beginning with the back. The fronts are picked up from the CO edge of the back at the shoulders and are knit separately until they are joined to the back at the underarms. After joining, the body is worked in one piece. The collar, front edgings, and armhole edgings are added once the body of the vest is complete.

If you are between sizes or wish to modify the bust size for any other reason, you may either add or subtract sts from the CO underarms, or you may knit the back from one size and the front from another size to customize the fit.

Textured Stitch Pattern (worked flat over an even [odd] number of sts)
Rows 1 and 3 (RS): K across.
Rows 2 and 4 (WS): P across.
Row 5: *K1, p1; rep from * to end, ending with k1 [p1].
Row 6: Knit the purl sts and purl the knit sts.
To work the Textured Stitch Pattern in the round, work Rnds 2 and 4 as: K across.
Rep Rows/Rnds 1-6 for pattern.

Make 1 Left (M1L)
Pick up the bar between st just worked and next st and place on needle as a regular stitch. Knit through the back loop.

Make 1 Right (M1R)
Pick up the bar between st just worked and next st and place on needle backwards (incorrect stitch mount). Knit through the front loop.

Make 1 Purl - Left (M1P-L)
Pick up the bar between st just worked and next st and place on needle backwards (incorrect stitch mount). Purl through the front loop.

Make 1 Purl - Right (M1P-R)
Pick up the bar between st just worked and next st and place on needle as a regular stitch. Purl through the back loop.

Backward Loop Cast On
With needle in your right hand, create a loop by passing the working yarn around your left thumb from back to front. Slip the needle tip under the loop around your thumb. Pull your thumb out of the loop and tug on the working yarn to tighten up the stitch. (For a video demonstration, see http://www.knitpicks.com/tutorials/Loop_Cast_On__D4.html).

DIRECTIONS

Modification Note: The Back for all four patterns is the same. To modify the neckline, complete the Back, then proceed to the first front in the pattern with the shaping you would like: the Shasta Vest for a V-neck, the Napali Cardigan for a high scoop worked flat, or the Yuri Pullover for a high scoop worked in the round.

Back

With longer circular needle, CO 54 (59, 64, 67, 68, 69, 70, 73, 74, 75) sts.
Purl 1 row (WS).
Beg with Row 1, work in Textured Stitch Pattern for 39 (35, 35, 33, 29, 25, 25, 25, 21, 19) row(s), or until piece measures 6.25 (5.5, 5.5, 5.25, 4.75, 4, 4, 4, 3.25, 3)", ending with a WS row.

Next Row, Armhole Inc Row (RS): K1, M1R, work in pat to last st, M1L, k1. 2 sts inc'd.

Working in Textured Stitch Pattern, rep Armhole Inc Row every 4th row 0 (2, 3, 2, 2, 2, 2, 2, 1, 1) more time(s), then every other row 2 (2, 2, 5, 8, 10, 12, 12, 17, 21) times, ending with a RS row. 60 (69, 76, 83, 90, 95, 100, 103, 112, 121) sts.

Last Armhole Inc Row (WS): P1, M1P-R, work in pat to last st, M1P-L, p1. 2 sts inc'd. 62 (71, 78, 85, 92, 97, 102, 105, 114, 123) sts.

Break yarn and place Back sts on spare needle, st holder, or scrap yarn.

Modification Note: If you would like to knit a pullover version of this vest, start with the Left Front and work through the row where sts are CO at the end of the row, but do not CO any sts. Place all Left Front sts on hold. Proceed to the Right Front and work up to the row just before the row where sts are CO at the end of the row. Next, follow the instructions in the Yuri Pullover pattern for joining the Right and Left Front (including the number of sts CO). Then work the fronts together, continuing the armhole shaping on both sides of your knitting. Join the Front to the Back as in the Yuri Pullover pattern, then proceed to the Body instructions in this pattern.

Right Front

With RS of Back facing, starting at the top right edge, and using longer circular needle, pick up 6 (8, 10, 11, 11, 11, 12, 12, 13, 13) sts from the CO edge.
Purl 1 row (WS).
Beg with Row 1, work in Textured Stitch Pattern for 10 (14, 18, 18, 18, 18, 20, 20, 20, 18) rows, or until piece measures 1.75 (2.5, 3, 3, 3, 3, 3.25, 3.25, 3.25, 3)", ending with a WS row.

Note: The armhole and scoop neck are shaped at the same time for most sizes. Please read the rest of this section in its entirety before proceeding and refer to the instructions broken down by size below to determine when to start each set of shaping.

Size 28.5":
Proceed to Deep Scoop Neck Shaping. After Deep Scoop Neck Shaping is complete, work 7 rows in Textured Stitch Pattern, then proceed to Armhole Shaping.

Size 32.5":
Proceed to Deep Scoop Neck Shaping. Begin Armhole Shaping on the last row of Deep Scoop Neck Shaping (when sts are CO at the end of the row).

Sizes 36.5", 40.5", 44.5", 52.5", and 56.5":
Proceed to Deep Scoop Shaping. Begin Armhole Shaping on the same row as the - (-, 7th, 6th, 4th, -, 2nd, 2nd, -, -) Deep Scoop increase.

Size 48.5":
Proceed to Deep Scoop Neck Shaping. Begin Armhole Shaping 2 rows after the 2nd Deep Scoop increase.

Size 60.5":
Begin Deep Scoop Neck Shaping and Armhole Shaping on the same row.

Size 64.5":
Proceed to Armhole Shaping. Begin Deep Scoop Neck Shaping 2 rows after the 1st Armhole increase.

Deep Scoop Neck Shaping

Next Row, Deep Scoop Inc Row (RS): Work in pat to last st, M1L, k1. 1 st inc'd.
Working in pat (and incorporating Armhole Inc Rows as necessary when the time comes), rep Deep Scoop Inc Row every 4th row 2 more times, then every other row 5 (5, 5, 6, 6, 6, 7, 7, 7) times.

Last Deep Scoop Inc Row (WS): P1, M1P-R, work in pat to end. 1 st inc'd.

Modification Note: For a vest that fastens in the front without overlap, only CO 10 (11, 11, 11, 11, 12, 11, 12, 11, 12) sts on the next row. To add lace to the front edge, CO 2 fewer sts, mark the last 12 sts of the row, and work Cellular Stitch from the Napali Cardigan pattern over those sts until the hem ribbing begins. To add a cable to the front edge, CO 2 additional sts on the next row, mark the last 12 sts of the row, and work the Shadow Cable from the Yuri Pullover pattern over those sts until the hem ribbing begins.

Note: If you intend to wear the vest hanging open and the WS will show, CO an extra 3 sts in the next row, then work those sts in Garter Stitch: K on every row. Then, omit the Front Edgings.

Next Row (RS): Work in pat to end (incorporating Armhole Inc's if necessary), then CO 20 (21, 21, 21, 21, 22, 21, 22, 21, 22) sts using the Backward Loop method. Total sts (including armhole shaping, if applicable): 35 (39, 42, 45, 47, 50, 51, 54, 57, 59).

Armhole Shaping

Armhole Inc Row (RS): K1, M1R, work in pat to end (incorporating deep scoop shaping if necessary). 1 st inc'd.
Working in pat and incorporating Deep Scoop Inc Rows as necessary, rep Armhole Inc Row every 4th row 0 (2, 3, 2, 2, 2, 2, 2, 1, 1) more time(s), then every other row 2 (2, 2, 5, 8, 10, 12, 12, 17, 21) times.

Last Armhole Inc Row (WS): Work in pat to last st, M1P-L, p1. 1 st inc'd. 39 (44, 47, 51, 54, 57, 59, 61, 65, 70) sts after all shaping and CO are complete.

Break yarn and place Right Front sts on spare needle, st holder, or scrap yarn.

Left Front

With RS of Back facing, count to the 6 (8, 10, 11, 11, 11, 12, 12, 13, 13)th st from the top left edge. With longer circular needle, pick up 6 (8, 10, 11, 11, 11, 12, 12, 13, 13) sts from the CO edge.
Purl 1 row (WS).
Beg with Row 1, work in Textured Stitch Pattern for 10 (14, 18, 18,

18, 18, 20, 20, 20, 18) rows, or until piece measures 1.75 (2.5, 3, 3, 3, 3.25, 3.25, 3.25, 3)", ending with a WS row.

Note: The armhole and scoop neck are shaped at the same time for most sizes. Please read the rest of this section in its entirety before proceeding and refer to the instructions broken down by size below to determine when to start each set of shaping.

Size 28.5" and 32.5":
Proceed to Deep Scoop Neck Shaping. After Deep Scoop Shaping is complete, work 8 (0, -, -, -, -, -, -, -, -) rows in Textured Stitch Pattern, then proceed to Armhole Shaping.

Sizes 36.5", 40.5", 44.5", 52.5", and 56.5":
Proceed to Deep Scoop Neck Shaping. Begin Armhole Shaping on the same row as the - (-, 7th, 6th, 4th, -, 2nd, 2nd, -, -) Deep Scoop Inc Row.

Size 48.5":
Proceed to Deep Scoop Neck Shaping. Begin Armhole Shaping 2 rows after the 2nd Deep Scoop Inc Row.

Size 60.5":
Begin Deep Scoop Neck Shaping and Armhole Shaping on the same row.

Size 64.5":
Proceed to Armhole Shaping. Begin Deep Scoop Shaping 2 rows after the 1st Armhole Inc Row.

Deep Scoop Neck Shaping

Next Row, Deep Scoop Inc Row (RS): K1, M1R, work in pat to end. 1 st inc'd.
Working in pat (and incorporating Armhole Inc Rows as necessary when the time comes), rep Deep Scoop Inc Row every 4th row 2 more times, then every other row 5 (5, 5, 6, 6, 6, 7, 7, 7) times.

Modification Note: For a vest that fastens in the front without overlap, only CO 10 (11, 11, 11, 11, 12, 11, 12, 11, 12) sts on the next row. To add lace to the front edge, CO 2 fewer sts, mark the first 12 sts of the next RS row, and work Cellular Stitch from the Napali Cardigan pattern over those sts until the hem ribbing begins. To add a cable to the front edge, CO 2 additional sts on the next row, mark the first 12 sts of the next RS row, and work the Shadow Cable from the Yuri Pullover pattern over those sts until the hem ribbing begins.

Note: If you intend to wear the vest hanging open and the WS will show, CO an extra 3 sts in the next row, then work those sts in Garter Stitch: K on every row. Then, omit the Front Edgings.

Last Deep Scoop Inc Row (WS): Work to last st, M1P-L, p1, then CO 20 (21, 21, 21, 21, 22, 21, 22, 21, 22) sts using the Backward Loop method. 35 (38, 41, 44, 46, 49, 50, 53, 56, 58) sts (including armhole shaping, if applicable).

Armhole Shaping

Armhole Inc Row (RS): Work in pat to last st (incorporating deep scoop shaping if necessary), M1L, k1. 1 st inc'd.
Working in pat and incorporating Deep Scoop Inc Rows as necessary, rep Armhole Inc Row every 4th row 0 (2, 3, 2, 2, 2,

2, 1, 1) more time(s), then every other row 2 (2, 2, 5, 8, 10, 12, 12, 17, 21) times.

Last Armhole Inc Row (WS): P1, M1P-R, work in pat to end. 1 st inc'd.39 (44, 47, 51, 54, 57, 59, 61, 65, 70) sts after all shaping and CO are complete.

Leave sts on your needle and do not break yarn.

Body

Join Fronts and Back (RS): Work in pat to end of Left Front, CO 2 (2, 4, 6, 8, 12, 16, 22, 22, 22) sts using Backward Loop Method, place sts of Back onto left hand needle, work in pat to end of Back, CO 2 (2, 4, 6, 8, 12, 16, 22, 22, 22) sts using Backward Loop Method, place sts of Right Front onto left hand needle, and work in pat to end of Right Front. 144 (163, 180, 199, 216, 235, 252, 271, 288, 307) sts.

Modification Note: To add waist shaping, see the Body instructions in the Napali Cardigan pattern (for subtle shaping), the Shasta Vest pattern (for a slightly more emphasized waist), or the Yuri Pullover pattern (for an empire waist). Continue to work in the Textured Stitch Pattern, rather than St st.

Work in Textured Stitch Pattern until Body measures 13.5 (13.5, 13.75, 14, 13.75, 13.75, 14, 14, 14, 14)", or 1 (1, 1, 1.25, 1.25, 1.25, 1.25, 1.5, 1.5)" less than desired length from underarm, ending with a WS row. On last row, inc 2 (1, 2, 1, 2, 1, 2, 1, 2, 1) st(s) anywhere in the row with M1L-P to make the st count compatible with the hem ribbing. 146 (164, 182, 200, 218, 236, 254, 272, 290, 308) sts.

Hem Ribbing (RS): *K2, p1; rep from * to last 2 sts, k2.
Work in ribbing pat as set in last rnd until ribbing measures 1 (1, 1, 1.25, 1.25, 1.25, 1.25, 1.5, 1.5)", ending with a WS row.

BO all sts knitwise.

Scoop Neck Edging

Modification Note: To add a large collar or turtleneck, see Turtleneck instructions in the Yuri Pullover pattern.

Beg at the top of the right front edge with RS facing and using longer circular needle, pick up 1 st for each st CO and roughly 3 sts for every 4 rows all the way around the neck opening. The exact number of sts is not important, but it should be a multiple of 3 sts plus 2.

Next Row, Ribbing (WS): *P2, k1; rep from * to last 2 sts, p2.

Work in ribbing pat as set in last row for 2 more rows.

BO all sts knitwise.

Front Edgings

Modification Note: To create button bands for a vest that fastens in the front without overlap, follow the instructions below for the left side. For the right side, see the Right Button Band instructions in the Napali Cardigan pattern.

Beg at the bottom of the right front opening or top of the left front opening with RS facing and using longer circular needle, PU roughly 3 sts for every 4 rows all the way up (or down) the vest opening. The exact number of sts is not important, but it should be a multiple of 3 sts plus 2.

Next Row (WS): *P2, k1; rep from * to last 2 sts, p2.

Work in ribbing pat as set in last row for 2 more rows.

BO all sts knitwise.

Armhole Edging

Modification Note: To add sleeves, follow the Sleeve instructions in the Yuri Pullover pattern (for 3/4 length) or in the Napali Cardigan pattern (for full length), continuing to work in the Textured Stitch Pattern rather than St st.

Starting in the center of the underarm, and using needles preferred for working a small circumference in the round, PU 1 st for each st CO and roughly 3 sts for every 4 rows all the way around the armhole opening. The exact number of sts is not important, but it should be a multiple of 3 sts. Pm, then join to work in the rnd.

Ribbing Rnd: *K2, p1; rep from * to end.
Work in ribbing pat as set in last rnd for 2 more rnds.

BO all sts knitwise.

Finishing

Weave in ends, wash and block to measurements in schematic.

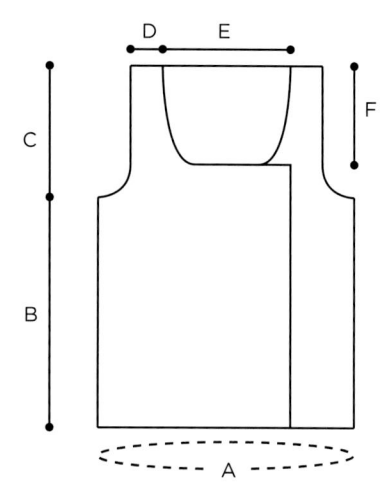

A 28.5 (32.5, 36.5, 40.5, 44.5, 48.5, 52.5, 56.5, 60.5, 64.5)" CLOSED
33 (37.25, 41, 45.25, 49, 53.25, 57, 61.25, 65, 69.25)" OPEN
B 14.5 (14.5, 14.75, 15, 15, 15, 15.25, 15.25, 15.5, 15.5)"
C 7.25 (8, 8.75, 8.75, 9, 9, 9.5, 9.5, 10, 11)"
D 1.25 (1.75, 2.25, 2.5, 2.5, 2.5, 2.75, 2.75, 3, 3)"
E 9.25 (9.5, 9.75, 10, 10.25, 10.5, 10.25, 11, 10.75, 11)"
F 5 (5.75, 6.5, 6.5, 6.75, 6.75, 7, 7.25, 7.25, 7.25)"

SHASTA VEST

FINISHED MEASUREMENTS
28.5 (32.5, 36.5, 40.5, 44.5, 48.5, 52.5, 56.5, 60.5, 64.5)" finished bust measurement; garment is meant to be worn with 0-2" of negative ease.

YARN
Knit Picks Swish Worsted (100% Superwash Merino Wool; 110 yards/50g):
Lost Lake Heather 25146, 5 (5, 5, 6, 7, 8, 8, 9, 9, 10) skeins.

NEEDLES
US 7 (4.5mm) 24-60" circular needles (length needed depends on size), 24"

circular needles (for collar), and DPNs or two 24" circular needles for two circulars technique, or one 32" or longer circular needle for Magic Loop technique, or size to obtain gauge

NOTIONS
Yarn Needle
2 Stitch Markers
Spare needle, stitch holders, or scrap yarn

GAUGE
18 sts and 25 rows = 4" in St st worked in the round, blocked.

Shasta Vest

Notes:
This simple pullover vest features a V-neck and waist shaping.

The vest is worked from the top down, beginning with the back. The fronts are picked up from the cast on edge of the back at the shoulders and are knit separately until they are joined at the bottom of the V-neck. The front and back are joined at the underarms, after which the body is worked in the round in one piece. The collar and armhole edgings are added once the body of the vest is complete.

If you are between sizes or wish to modify the bust size for any other reason, you may either add or subtract sts from the underarm cast on, or you may knit the back from one size and the front from another size to customize the fit.

Make 1 Left (M1L)
Pick up the bar between st just worked and next st and place on needle as a regular stitch. Knit through the back loop.

Make 1 Right (M1R)
Pick up the bar between st just worked and next st and place on needle backwards (incorrect stitch mount). Knit through the front loop.

Make 1 Purl - Left (M1P-L)
Pick up the bar between st just worked and next st and place on needle backwards (incorrect stitch mount). Purl through the front loop.

Make 1 Purl - Right (M1P-R)
Pick up the bar between st just worked and next st and place on needle as a regular stitch. Purl through the back loop.

Backward Loop Cast On
With needle in your right hand, create a loop by passing the working yarn around your left thumb from back to front. Slip the needle tip under the loop around your thumb. Pull your thumb out of the loop and tug on the working yarn to tighten up the stitch. (For a video demonstration, see http://www.knitpicks.com/tutorials/Loop_Cast_On__D4.html).

sl2 k1 p2sso
Slip 2 sts together as if to knit, k1, then pass the 2 slipped sts over the knit st.

DIRECTIONS

Modification Note: The Back for all four patterns is the same. To modify the neckline, complete the Back, then proceed to the first front in the pattern with the shaping you would like: the Moab Vest for a deep scoop, the Napali Cardigan for a high scoop worked flat, or the Yuri Pullover for a high scoop worked in the round.

Back

Modification Note: To add a lace panel down the back, CO 2 fewer sts than listed below, mark the center 21 sts, then work Cellular Stitch (from the Napali Cardigan pattern) over those 21 sts until the hem ribbing begins at the bottom of the sweater. To add a cable down the back, CO 2 additional sts, mark the center 12 sts, then work the Shadow Cable (from the Yuri Pullover pattern) over those 12 sts until the hem ribbing begins.

With longer circular needle, CO 54 (59, 64, 67, 68, 69, 70, 73, 74, 75) sts.

Work in St st (K on RS, P on WS) for 39 (35, 35, 33, 29, 25, 25, 25, 21, 19) rows, or until piece measures 6.25 (5.5, 5.5, 5.25, 4.75, 4, 4, 4, 3.25, 3)", beg and ending with a WS row.

Next Row, Armhole Inc Row (RS): K1, M1R, k to last st, M1L, k1. 2 sts inc'd.
Working in St st, rep Armhole Inc Row every 4th row 0 (2, 3, 2, 2, 2, 2, 2, 1, 1) more time(s), then every other row 2 (2, 2, 5, 8, 10, 12, 12, 17, 21) times. 60 (69, 76, 83, 90, 95, 100, 103, 112, 121) sts.

Last Armhole Inc Row (WS): P1, M1P-R, p to last st, M1P-L, p1. 2 sts inc'd. 62 (71, 78, 85, 92, 97, 102, 105, 114, 123) sts.

Break yarn and place Back sts on spare needle, st holder, or scrap yarn.

Modification Note: If you would like to knit an open version of this vest that can button in the front, start with the Right Front and omit the last two V-Neck Inc Rows. Work 4 rows in St st (incorporating armhole shaping if necessary), then proceed to the instructions for the Front, continuing the armhole shaping and omitting the joining row. Continue the armhole shaping as written for the right side of the front only and, once armhole shaping is complete, place Right Front sts on hold. Knit the Left Front as instructed, omitting the last two V-Neck Inc Rows. Work 4 rows in St st as for the Right Front and proceed to the Front, working the armhole shaping as written for the left side only. To join to the back, follow the joining instructions in the Napali Cardigan pattern, then proceed to the Body instructions in this pattern.

Left Front

With RS of Back facing, count to the 6 (8, 10, 11, 11, 11, 12, 12, 13, 13)th st from the top left edge. Starting here, with longer circular needle, pick up 6 (8, 10, 11, 11, 11, 12, 12, 13, 13) sts from the CO edge. Work in St st for 3 rows, beg and ending with a WS row.

Note: The armhole and V-neck are shaped at the same time. Please read the rest of this section in its entirety before proceeding.

V-Neck Shaping
Next Row, V-Neck Inc Row (RS): K1, M1R, k to end. 1 st inc'd.
Working in St st (and incorporating Armhole Inc Rows as necessary when the time comes), rep V-Neck Inc Row every 4th row 0 (1, 2, 2, 3, 3, 3, 3, 3, 3) more time(s), then every other row 19 (18, 18, 18, 18, 18, 19, 19, 19) times.

Armhole Shaping
AT THE SAME TIME, on the same row as the 19 (16, 15, 14, 11, 9, 9, 9, 7, 6)th V-Neck increase, beg armhole shaping.
Armhole Inc Row (RS): K to last st (incorporating V-Neck Inc Row), M1L, k1. 1 st inc'd.
Working in St st and incorporating V-Neck Inc Rows as necessary, rep Armhole Inc Row every 4th row 0 (2, 3, 2, 2, 2, 2, 2, 1, 1) more time(s), then every other row 1 (0, 0, 3, 7, 9, 9, 10, 14, 15) time(s). Total sts (including V-Neck Inc's): 28 (31, 35, 38, 43, 45, 46, 48, 52, 53).

Work one WS row after last increase.

Break yarn and place Left Front sts on spare needle, st holder, or scrap yarn.

Right Front

With RS of Back facing, starting at the top right edge, and using longer circular needle, pick up 6 (8, 10, 11, 11, 11, 12, 12, 13, 13) sts from the CO edge.

Work in St st for 3 rows, beg and ending with a WS row.

Note: The armhole and V-neck are shaped at the same time. Please read the rest of this section in its entirety before proceeding.

V-Neck Shaping

Next Row, V-Neck Inc Row (RS): K to last st, M1L, k1. 1 st inc'd.
Working in St st (and incorporating Armhole Inc Rows as necessary when the time comes), rep V-Neck Inc Row every 4th row 0 (1, 2, 2, 3, 3, 3, 3, 3) more time(s), then every other row 19 (18, 18, 18, 18, 18, 18, 19, 19, 19) times.

Armhole Shaping

AT THE SAME TIME, on the same row as the 19 (16, 15, 14, 11, 9, 9, 9, 7, 6)th V-Neck increase, beg armhole shaping.

Armhole Inc Row (RS): K1, M1R, k to end (incorporating V-Neck Inc Row). 1 st inc'd.
Working in St st and incorporating V-Neck Inc Rows as necessary, rep Armhole Inc Row every 4th row 0 (2, 3, 2, 2, 2, 2, 2, 1, 1) more time(s), then every other row 1 (0, 0, 3, 7, 9, 9, 10, 14, 15) time(s). Total sts (including V-Neck Inc's): 28 (31, 35, 38, 43, 45, 46, 48, 52, 53).

Work one WS row after last increase.

Leave sts on your needle and do not break yarn.

Front

Next Row (RS): Join Right and Left Front, continuing armhole and V-neck shaping: K1, M1R, k to last st of Right Front, M1L, k1, CO 0 (1, 0, 1, 0, 1, 0, 1, 0, 1) st(s) using Backward Loop method, place sts of Left Front onto left hand needle, k1, M1R, k to last st, M1L, k1. 60 (67, 74, 81, 90, 95, 96, 101, 108, 111) sts.

Modification Note: To add a lace panel down the front of this vest, place markers on either side of the center 21 sts, then work Cellular Stitch (from the Napali Cardigan pattern) over those marked 21 sts until the hem ribbing begins. To add a cable down the front, mark the center 12 sts and work the Shadow Cable (from the Yuri Pullover) pattern over those sts until the hem ribbing begins. Adding lace will add 0.5" to the final bust measurement and adding the cable will remove 0.5", you may add or subtract 2 sts from the underarm CO to fix this.

Sizes – (32.5", 36.5", 40.5", -, -, 52.5", 56.5", 60.5", 64.5") ONLY:
Next Row (WS): P across.
Next Row (RS): K1, M1R, k to last st, M1L, k1. 2 sts inc'd.
Rep last 2 rows - (0, 0, 0, -, -, 1, 0, 1, 4) more time(s). - (69, 76, 83, -, -,100, 103, 112, 119) sts.

All Sizes:
Last Armhole Inc Row (WS): P1, M1P-R, purl to last st, M1P-L, p1. 62 (71, 78, 85, 92, 97, 102, 105, 114, 123) sts.

Body

Join Front and Back (RS): K to end of Front, CO 1 (1, 2, 3, 4, 6, 8, 11, 11, 11) st(s) using Backward Loop Method, pm, CO 1 (1, 2, 3, 4, 6, 8, 11, 11, 11) more st(s), place sts of Back onto left hand needle, k to end of Back, CO 1 (1, 2, 3, 4, 6, 8, 11, 11, 11) st(s) using Backward Loop Method, pm to mark beg of rnd, CO 1 (1, 2, 3, 4, 6, 8, 11, 11, 11) more st(s), and join to work in the rnd. 128 (146, 164, 182, 200, 218, 236, 254, 272, 290) sts.

Modification Note: To alter the waist shaping, see the Body instructions in the Moab Vest pattern (for no waist shaping), the Napali Cardigan pattern (for a subtler waist), or the Yuri Pullover pattern (for an empire waist). If working flat, replace the Waist Dec Rnds below with the Waist Dec Row from the Napali Cardigan pattern.

Work in St st for 11 rnds, or until piece measures 2" from underarm.

Next Rnd, Waist Dec Rnd: *K1, ssk, k to 2 sts before marker, k2tog, sm; rep from * once more. 4 sts dec'd.

Working in St st, rep Waist Dec Rnd when Body measures 4.5 (4.5, 4.5, 4.5, 4.5, 4.5, 4.75, 4.75, 4.75, 4.75)" from underarm, then again when Body measures 7 (7, 7.25, 7.25, 7.25, 7.25, 7.5, 7.5, 7.5, 7.5)" from underarm. 116 (134, 152, 170, 188, 206, 224, 242, 260, 278) sts.

Work in St st for 5 rnds.

Next Rnd, Hip Inc Rnd: *K1, M1R, k to marker, M1L, sm; rep from * once more. 4 sts inc'd.

Working in St st, rep Hip Inc Rnd every 10th rnd 3 more times. 132 (150, 168, 186, 204, 222, 240, 258, 276, 294) sts.

Work in St st until Body measures 13.5 (13.5, 13.75, 13.75, 13.75, 13.75, 14, 14, 14, 14)", or 1.5 (1.5, 1.5, 1.5, 1.75, 1.75, 1.75, 1.75, 2, 2)" less than desired length from underarm.

Hem Ribbing: *K2, p1; rep from * to end.
Work in ribbing pat as set in last rnd until ribbing measures 1.5 (1.5, 1.5, 1.5, 1.75, 1.75, 1.75, 1.75, 2, 2)".

BO all sts knitwise.

V-Neck Edging

Modification Note: If knitting an open version of this vest, pick up sts (a multiple of 3 plus 2) around the collar opening beginning at the right front edge. Working in the ribbing pat below, dec 1 st at each edge for 3 rows before binding off.

Beg where the front meets the back at the right shoulder with RS facing and using 24" circular needles, PU 76 (79, 82, 85, 88, 88, 88, 91, 91, 91) sts (or a multiple of 3 sts plus 1) across the back neck and down the left front (this will be 1 st per st CO at the back neck and roughly 3 sts per 4 rows down the left front), pm, PU 1 st at the very bottom of the v-neck where the two fronts meet, then PU 35 (38, 41, 41, 44, 44, 44, 44, 44, 44) sts (or a multiple of 3 sts plus 2) up the right front (roughly 3 sts per 4 rows). 112 (118, 124, 127, 133, 133, 133, 136, 136, 136) sts. Pm to mark beg of rnd, then join to work in the rnd.

Next Rnd: *K2, p1; rep from * to 1 st before marker, sl2-k1-p2sso, removing marker as you come to it and replacing it before the newly formed st, p1, *k2, p1; rep from * to end. 2 sts dec'd.

Next Rnd: Work in ribbing pat as established in last row to 1 st before marker, sl2-k1-p2sso, removing marker as you come to it and replacing it before the newly formed st, then work in ribbing pat as established to end. 2 sts dec'd.
Rep last rnd once more.

BO all sts knitwise.

Armhole Edging

Modification Note: To add sleeves, follow the Sleeve instructions in the Yuri Pullover pattern (for 3/4 length) or in the Napali Cardigan pattern (for full length).

Starting in the center of the underarm, and using needles preferred for working a small circumference in the round, PU 1 st for each st CO and roughly 3 sts for every 4 rows all the way around the armhole opening. The exact number of sts is not important, but it should be a multiple of 3. Pm, then join to work in the rnd.

Ribbing: *K2, p1; rep from * to end.
Work in ribbing pat as set in last rnd for 2 more rnds..
BO all sts knitwise.

Finishing

Weave in ends, wash and block to measurements in schematic.

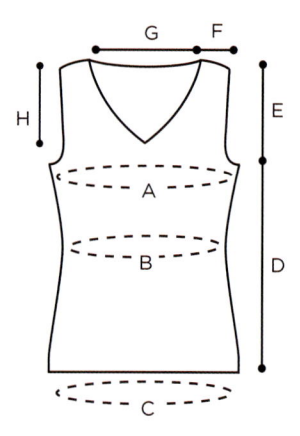

A 28.5 (32.5, 36.5, 40.5, 44.5, 48.5, 52.5, 56.5, 60.5, 64.5)"
B 25.75 (29.75, 33.75, 37.75, 41.75, 45.75, 49.75, 53.75, 57.75, 61.75)"
C 29.25 (33.25, 37.25, 41.25, 45.25, 49.25, 53.25, 57.25, 61.25, 65.25)"
D 15 (15, 15.25, 15.25, 15.5, 15.75, 15.75, 15.75, 16, 16)"
E 7.25 (8, 8.75, 8.75, 9, 9, 9.5, 9.5, 10, 11)"
F 1.25(1.75, 2.25, 2.5, 2.5, 2.5, 2.5 2.75, 2.75, 3, 3)"
G 9.25 (9.5, 9.75, 10, 10.25, 10.5, 10.25, 11, 10.75, 11)"
H 7 (7.25, 8, 8, 8.75, 8.75, 8.75, 9, 9, 9)"

For pattern support, contact xilary@gmail.com

Abbreviations								
BO	bind off	M	marker		stitch	TBL	through back loop
cn	cable needle	M1	make one stitch	RH	right hand	TFL	through front loop
CC	contrast color	M1L	make one left-leaning	rnd(s)	round(s)	tog	together
CDD	Centered double dec		stitch	RS	right side	W&T	wrap & turn (see
CO	cast on	M1R	make one right-lean-	Sk	skip		specific instructions
cont	continue		ing stitch	Sk2p	sl 1, k2tog, pass		in pattern)
dec	decrease(es)	MC	main color		slipped stitch over	WE	work even
DPN(s)	double pointed	P	purl		k2tog: 2 sts dec	WS	wrong side
	needle(s)	P2tog	purl 2 sts together	SKP	sl, k, psso: 1 st dec	WYIB	with yarn in back
EOR	every other row	PM	place marker	SL	slip	WYIF	with yarn in front
inc	increase	PFB	purl into the front and	SM	slip marker	YO	yarn over
K	knit		back of stitch	SSK	sl, sl, k these 2 sts tog		
K2tog	knit two sts together	PSSO	pass slipped stitch	SSP	sl, sl, p these 2 sts tog		
KFB	knit into the front and		over		tbl		
	back of stitch	PU	pick up	SSSK	sl, sl, sl, k these 3 sts		
K-wise	knitwise	P-wise	purlwise		tog		
LH	left hand	rep	repeat	St st	stockinette stitch		
		Rev St st	reverse stockinette	sts	stitch(es)		

Knit Picks yarn is both luxe and affordable—a seeming contradiction trounced! But it's not just about the pretty colors; we also care deeply about fiber quality and fair labor practices, leaving you with a gorgeously reliable product you'll turn to time and time again.

THIS COLLECTION FEATURES

SWISH WORSTED
WORSTED WEIGHT
100% SUPERWASH MERINO

View these beautiful yarns and more at www.KnitPicks.com